To my mom and dad,
who are the best

Fit to Burst

ABUNDANCE, MAYHEM, AND THE
JOYS OF MOTHERHOOD

Rachel Jankovic

canonpress
Moscow, Idaho

Published by Canon Press
P.O. Box 8729, Moscow, Idaho 83843
800.488.2034 | www.canonpress.com

Rachel Jankovic, *Fit to Burst:*
Abundance, Mayhem, and the Joys of Motherhood

Cover design by Rachel Rosales.
Interior design by Laura Storm Design.
Printed in the United States of America.

Scripture taken from the King James Version.

Library of Congress Cataloging-in-Publication Data
Jankovic, Rachel.
  Fit to burst : abundance, mayhem, and the joys of motherhood / by Rachel Jankovic.
      p. cm.
  ISBN 978-1-59128-128-3
1. Mothers--Religious life. 2. Motherhood--Religious aspects--Christianity. 3. Generosity--Religious aspects--Christianity. 4. Sacrifice--Christianity. I. Title.
  BV4529.18.J365 2013
  248.8'431--dc23
                                    2012043111

15 16 17 18   9 8 7 6 5 4 3

Contents

Foreword

I'll tell you the truth about this book. It seems only fair since, apparently, you are sitting with it in your hands, about to dive in. If I were a great mother, this book would not be here. If I always knew what to do with my kids—if it all came easily—there would have been nothing to say. You don't have to wrestle with issues if you aren't struggling with them, after all.

Many of the things I write about are quite current for me, and they will be tomorrow, too. Having thought of a way to deal with something does not take care of that issue forever. I will continue to have to practice the things I write about, and that is good.

I don't pull punches or hold back in this book, because I am writing to myself as much as to you. I know that as mothers we face very similar temptations, and we have a unique opportunity to sympathize with each other over those challenges. We have a common bond.

We are the sisterhood of the people who know about long days. That is true. But the fact that we all face the same temptations should give us a burning desire to conquer them, not to wallow in them. I write hard-hitting things to myself, because I want to grow in grace. I'm sharing them with you in the hopes that they will strengthen your faith and encourage you to mother in a way that honors Christ.

If something in this book strikes a little close to home for you, know that it struck in my home first. I am not writing about other people's problems, although I know many of them are common. I write about what I know, and what I know is the challenges, the joys, the work that is involved in raising little people.

If you don't want to be challenged, then don't read this book. If you are just looking for sympathy and an eye-roll about the work you do, just mention you have children to someone at the grocery store.

This book is a collection of "field notes" from a mom seeking to honor the Lord in her daily life. It isn't a method or a system, because it is messy, just like the life I am busy living.

I write quickly, in a short amount of time. I write during my normal life, with my kids doing the normal thing. I write with a toddler on my lap or type with one hand while I nurse my sweet new boy. I am not pretending to be a mother, writing about motherhood in the abstract—I am writing about what is very real to me.

I hope you can hear my little people in the background of this book. I hope you can hear them playing, telling me they are thirsty, or periodically interrupting for snacks. I hope you can hear that we are making playdough, or dealing with someone who is crying.

Since I wrote *Loving the Little Years*, my children have grown a little. What I write about has grown a little bit too. But it is built on the same foundation— grace, grace, and more grace. I hope that it will encourage you in some way.

CHAPTER ONE

The Paradox Perspective

Before you dive into this book, I'd like to make sure that I am perfectly clear about a few things. As you read, you will notice a lot of emphasis on giving and sacrifice. To keep the whole book from becoming one huge parenthetical remark, I'd like to discuss this at the outset. The mentality of sacrifice is not a mentality of sorrow. The life of giving is not an empty life. I am not writing about sacrifice because I think that moms as a whole are not run-down enough, or tired enough, or working hard enough. I write about it because it is the first step to encouragement, to clearing your mind, to being fulfilled.

Scripture is very clear on this—if you seek to be full, give. The verse about the first being last and the last being first is not talking about how all the winners will be losers at the end. As though life were a footrace and at the end a little surprise switcheroo happens—the officials declare, "Actually, this was not about being first! We just wanted to see who was the slowest and give them the prize!"

Rather, this verse is talking about those who seek their own interests first. Those who put themselves above others will be the last. Those who value themselves the least will be the most valued. There isn't any way to do this other than the hard way. Giving with a lot of enthusiasm for watching yourself in the mirror isn't really giving, it is just watching yourself. Sacrifice isn't really sacrifice if it involves only doing what you want.

The point I want to make is that this is not my tricky innovation; it is a principle of Christian living. It is easy for us to mishear and to be offended by this kind of talk, because it is not the way the world thinks.

Most of us grew up in a culture that despises this kind of thinking, and it may not come naturally to us. But we need to have the language of Scripture define our way of thinking, and not truisms from the world.

Many of us might hear, "Sacrifice for your children every day," and immediately think, "But who is looking out for *me*? I have needs!" Let's consider a sampling of verses from Scripture that pertain to giving ourselves.

> Give, and it shall be given unto you; good measure, pressed down, and shaken together, and running over, shall men give into your lap. For with the same measure that you measure it shall be measured to you again. (Lk. 6:38)

This is my commandment, That ye love one another, as I have loved you. Greater love hath no man than this, that a man lay down his life for his friends. Ye are my friends, if ye do whatsoever I command you. (Jn. 15:12–15)

Let nothing be done through strife or vainglory; but in lowliness of mind let each esteem other better than themselves. Look not every man on his own things, but every man also on the things of others. (Phil. 2:3–4)

There is that scatters, and yet increases; and there is that withholds more than is right, but it leads to poverty. (Prov. 11:24)

The more we are steeped in the language of the Bible, the more we will recognize when things from the world are slipping in. When you find yourself getting stuck in a needing mentality, you will look for ways to give. And you won't look for ways to give just because you have to, and it is a terrible Christian duty. It *is* our duty, but when we faithfully obey as unto the Lord, we are given great joy, great satisfaction, and great fulfillment in the task. When you empty yourself for others, God fills you up. But not so you can suddenly retire with your little packet of joy. God gives to us that we may give. We give, He gives us more, with which to give more. It is not a cycle that will stop as soon as our kids turn eighteen. This is God's pattern for the life of believers whether or not they have children. This is how He wants us to be as people. Not just as mothers.

If you are like me, then motherhood may be the first time you were really tested in the business of laying down your life. I am not saying that I never did anything hard before I became a mother, but motherhood is different. For one, most other challenges that I had experience with ended. Motherhood is not just a job, it is an identity. More importantly, it is an identity that begins and ends with giving.

Being a mother changes your role in the world. Here are these little people, and they need you. They will go on needing you every day, for life. They change what you can do, where you can go, how you sleep. They get up in the gears of every part of your life. You may have given up a career to have children. You have given up your body. You may want to think that whatever you've given up was enough. *The sacrifice can stop already because look at what I've already lost. Don't ask more of me, I have given it all.*

There are two things about this that bear mentioning. First, there is a difference between giving something and having it taken from you. If you still count the things that you lost with resentment, then you did not give them. You need to let go of those things that you no longer have. Lay them down. If you find yourself in bed at night tallying what has been lost to you, you need to let go of that list. Lay them down. Give them freely. Don't count them as stolen.

The second thing I hope we can see is found in the second chapter of Philippians. These verses are probably quite familiar to you, and that makes it easy to skim past without really thinking about what they say, so slow down and read with specific application to your role as a mother:

> Let nothing be done through strife or vainglory; but in lowliness of mind let each esteem other better than themselves. Look not every man on his own things, but every man also on the things of others. (vv. 3–4)

This passage begins with this exhortation about how we are to view others. "Others" most certainly includes your children. Prioritize their needs. Think their needs are more important than yours.

And it continues: Why should we do this? Because we are to imitate Christ. Let *this* mind be in us:

> Let this mind be in you, which was also in Christ Jesus: Who, being in the form of God, thought it not robbery to be equal with God: But made himself of no reputation, and took upon him the form of a servant, and was made in the likeness of men: And being found in fashion as a man, he humbled himself, and became obedient unto death, even the death of the cross. (vv. 5–8)

There is no amount of humbling ourselves that can compare to Christ's death. Whatever hot thoughts you can come up with about cleaning the bathroom or dealing with the sick children or wiping the snot off your shirt, whatever it is, it isn't much. We were already fallen creatures before we took on motherhood. But this passage calls us to imitate Christ in this. Have you taken on the form of a servant? Have you made yourself of no reputation? That should sound familiar at least. This is how we imitate Christ: We esteem others greater than ourselves, and that turns into action. You will be humbled. You will have opportunities to humble yourself further. Choose to do so gladly, not resentfully.

Christ's life given up for others is the centerpiece of our faith. Our lives given up for others is the centerpiece of our faithfulness. The glory is that, in both cases, death is not the end. Christ has died for us for all time. But the trail He blazed does not end in the grave. He tells us to follow, to imitate Him.

This book is about that. About giving. About sacrifice. About humbling yourself. About valuing others. But primarily it is about life. It is about sinking your teeth into the kinds of moments that motherhood offers you. It is about growing in Christ in the mundane. It is about seeing the gospel in the work you are doing. It is about joy and faith and laughter beyond the sacrifice.

CHAPTER TWO

The Unbaked Biscuit

I've had this thing going lately about biscuits. It is probably due to the colder (delicious) fall air. This is the season of comfort food. But to have comfort food, there needs to be a comfort person. This is not just the season to have a hot dinner hitting the table, it is the season to have a person who loves you putting it there. In my life (prompted by the cute faces that travel about my home at half height) this has somehow become a burning need to perfect biscuits. Of course there are other things too, but biscuits are just so symbolic.

Biscuits make up a small part of the culinary world. They are easy and quick, and have been satisfying children leaving honey trails on the table for generations. But biscuits have to be made. It isn't enough to think of biscuits, because having thought of them doesn't make a childhood more full. Having thought of them doesn't give the dinner table that wonderful allure that having actually made them does. Your thoughts alone will not play into the memories of your children.

A little guilt cycle often happens in the life of a mother. It usually goes something like this, and could take anywhere from two minutes to two years to complete itself:

I thought of biscuits. I would like to be a person who makes biscuits for my hungry children. I do not feel like making biscuits right now. I will make biscuits another time. I will have time when I am not tired and feeling fat. The kids won't know. I wish I had made biscuits. I could have made biscuits. I'm such a bad mom who doesn't make biscuits. I am not as good as all the moms who are everywhere in this stupid world making biscuits. People who talk about making biscuits are self-righteous. I hate biscuits. They make me feel guilty. Jesus loves me! Biscuits or not! Jesus doesn't care that I didn't make biscuits. Home free! Biscuit-free!

Of course the conclusion here is perfectly accurate. Jesus doesn't care in the abstract whether or not you are making biscuits. And of course biscuits are only an example of something that you could do for your children, might not want to do, wish you had done, and then feel stricken with guilt over not doing. It could just as easily be decorating your kids' room, sewing a dress, making the birthday cake they wanted, talking to them in the evening longer than you wanted to, quitting your job to prioritize spending time with them, cleaning the bathroom, or any other thing that could actually be done—anything that could qualify as a work.

The thing is, works-righteousness is a damning theology. Jesus did the work for us by living sinlessly and dying for our sins. We cannot earn anything by doing, so it is dangerous to start talking about anything that Christians *should* be doing. If you could be the most accomplished mother in the world on your own strength, it wouldn't matter in the end. There is no freedom from sin that you can find by doing something. Jesus is all. His blood is sufficient, and there is nothing you can do that will change that.

But His blood will change you. When Jesus is all, things happen. When you believe to your core that you are forgiven and loved, one of the first things that happens is you start doing things. Fruit is intimately connected with forgiveness. When we are forgiven, we do not gallop out into a life of ambiguity and indifference. We do not become great negotiators of whether or not it matters that we aren't doing things. We become filled with gratitude, love, joy, and peace. And then, having a firm foundation of another's righteousness, we are free to go out and *do*.

Jesus does not care even the tiniest bit what you do for your salvation, because there is nothing you can do for it. But He cares very much what you do *with* it. Having been given it, go out and . . . reflect on all the things that you don't have to do? be embittered by every appearance of work? despise anything that doesn't come easily to you, that might be difficult? choose to be above the physical world? look down on sisters who are getting more done than you?

What is fruit but the outworking of our salvation? Take what you have been given, and turn a profit on it. The parable of the talents in Matthew 25 is quite relevant here. The master gives gold to his servants before he leaves on a journey. Two of them use the gold to earn more. Their investment pleases the master. He says, "Well done!" But the man who is given one talent and merely keeps it safe does not please him. "Why would you bury what I gave you? Why would you sit on it in fear? What I gave you was to be used. Turn a profit on it."

Is this us? Are we always guarding the gold we were given, always afraid of losing something? Are we storing up an arsenal of unbaked biscuits with which we will feed no one? And when our Master returns and asks us, "What have you done with what I have given you?" will we point at the other servants and say, "Look at them! They thought the gold you gave us wasn't sufficient. I knew it was, so I hid it, to keep it safe for Your return"?

Our Master did not give us this gold of forgiveness so that we might hide it. He wants us to use it. He wants us to make things happen with it. He wants us to take our salvation and turn it into biscuits, hot on the table. He wants us to take our salvation and turn it into contagious joy, into sacrifice for others. He wants us to use it.

The love of Christ is not the reason that we don't have to do things. It is the reason we get to do things freely. If you had no gold, there would have been nothing to invest. If your Master gave you gold, you should not be sitting on it.

In Christian circles there is constant talk about free salvation. It *is* free, thank God. But it is only free to *us*. *God* paid a great price for it. Jesus paid with His blood. It is free to us because someone else paid a great deal. And this is why we do not work out our salvation by never doing anything that might be hard or difficult to us. We imitate Christ, and we make sacrifices for others. We do things that are hard, that cost us much, *because* we want our gifts to be *free* to others.

It is so easy for us as mothers to look at the work we do on behalf of our families and resent that it is free to them. *Look at those kids, thinking that the clean clothes just appear magically. Look at these people, not valuing the cost of my work. Look at this ungrateful family who just takes the food and eats it. Like it was free!* But it is very important that we see the damage that this kind of thinking brings with it.

When we want the cost to be shared by all, we are not imitating Christ. When we imitate Christ, we want to give what costs us much, and we want to give it freely. Of course we have short-term vision, and often we feel like when we freely give, we need to see right away that it is being used responsibly. We worry that our free sacrifice will make our children greedy takers.

We think that we can see how wrong it would be if they thought that our making of biscuits was in any way easy. We want to know, within the next fifteen minutes, that everyone saw what we sacrificed, acknowledged it gratefully, thanked us profusely, reflected on it quietly, and came up with a way to repay us. But God thinks in much, much bigger story lines.

So imitate Christ in your giving. Do it daily, do it in as many little ways as you possibly can. Find a way to imitate Him in the folding of the laundry, in the stocking of the fridge, in the picking up of other people's socks. And then decide consciously that you are giving this meal, this clean room, this cheerful Christmas— that you are giving it all freely. And much later, maybe thirty years later, you would like to see your children turn a profit on it. You would like to see your kids taking what they were freely given and turning it into still more free giving. This is because God's story is never little. He works in generations, in lifetimes, and He wants us to do the same.

So if the very suggestion of something you might *do* makes you bristle, if it makes you feel judged or threatened or angry, you need to look to Christ. Your salvation has been paid for; this isn't about that. Stop and be grateful. Thank God things to bake have nothing to do with your salvation. Thank Him for loving you. Thank Him that He has given you so much to use. Then, after you have remembered the strength of your salvation, go out and do something with it. Find ways to use what you have been given to freely bless those around you. Tie on an apron and dust yourself lightly with flour. You are not here in this world to work your salvation *in* (thank God), you are here to work it *out*.

There are a million different ways to use this kind of gold. As much as God wants us to be using it, He wants us to be using it in different ways. We don't all need to be making biscuits, but we should all be doing something. We should be getting our hands into stuff to give. We should be blessing others, thinking of others, giving to others. And we should be doing it so freely that we don't remember it, because we are willing to wait to see what is done with it. We are willing to see, years down the road, what kind of interest accrued on those biscuits.

CHAPTER THREE

The Mean Boss

One evening a while ago I was talking with my husband after the kids had all gone to bed. We were just talking about how things were going and what we needed to work on. I found myself giving him a review of all the things that I was not getting done. I specifically remember bringing up the state of the upstairs bathroom. I had not even gotten close to cleaning it in a long time. I was so grossed out by the dirtiness of the bathroom, and I was being quite hard-core about my own failure to clean it. There were other things, too—I wanted the yard to look nice, the playroom to be organized, the bedding to all be clean and darling, and so on and such forth.

It just hit me all of the sudden how funny it was that I was sitting there complaining about my own job performance. And I was telling my husband all of the ways I was better than this. Not in those words of course. I was just itemizing the things I hadn't gotten to with a critical spirit. I was picking on myself, but I was doing it with part of myself that didn't want to take any responsibility for happened.

That critical, complaining part of me was the mean boss. The part of me that failed to get it done during the course of the day was the employee. In this particular situation, I was bringing out the mean boss in order to make the employee look bad. *It was her fault! I clearly expect a lot more of her. She is a failure. Let me take a moment to distance my leadership from her performance.*

Anyway, I realized suddenly that this was at the heart of the constant tension in my work at home. I am in charge both of setting the goals and expectations, and of following through on them. I am both the boss and the employee. It can be phrased another way that may feel more familiar to many of you: How can you care enough to try, but not so much that you lose it when you fail? How can you be motivated to work hard on something that will, in all likelihood, fall apart sometime in the near future? How can you aspire to have a productive Saturday, but hold it loosely when it doesn't happen? How can you both work diligently on a to-do list and cheerfully lay it down when you are interrupted?

This is where we can easily put on the persona of a beat-up employee. *I tried, but I'm not good enough to do it. I was working on that, but things just kept happening and I lost track of it. I wanted to get the house together today but I didn't because I am like that. I am a failure. I can't do anything. I should clearly be fired.*

When I was itemizing that trouble with the upstairs bathroom, it finally occurred to me that my husband actually did not care. He would doubtless have preferred a cheerful welcome to our messy home than a numbered list of things I intended to do. So what exactly was going on here? I realized that I was telling him about my expectations. And apparently my expectations were not aware of what my life is actually like. My expectations were ignoring—intentionally, too—that I had spent the day with a toddler. And that a mountain of laundry had been tamed. My expectations ignored the dinner that was served. They pretended not to notice the clean children or all the dishes that had been done that day. They turned a blind eye to the baby that was (at that time) growing inside. My expectations were a seriously mean boss.

When you are a mother and a homemaker, you are your own boss. The days are what you make of them. The tasks that need to get done are put on a list at your discretion. This means that you must be leadership material.

At the same time, what you get done is up to you, too. You also have to be a hardworking employee. The part of you that decides where to go must work with the part of you that needs to go there. Making a list that you cannot accomplish does not make you a better housewife, it makes you a bad leader. Snarking at yourself just makes you a bad leader who is also mean.

There are a lot of different combinations that can happen here. Sometimes you are a really great employee, but a bummer of a leader. You can set the standards for yourself so low that you will always achieve them with time left over. But where are you going? What do you aspire to? Who has a vision around here? If the leader in you is happy for you to spend the days in your pajamas, then the leader in you needs to wake up.

Sometimes you might be a bad leader the other way. You set the standards for yourself based on some sort of mythical time when children didn't get dirt under their fingernails. In this life there is nothing for you but discouragement, because no matter what you do, you cannot conform your performance to your expectations. This would probably manifest in your life most often as you succumb to discontent, discouragement, and despair. Or it may manifest itself by making you an absolutely no fun person to be around. Your children fear the wrath of leaving finger oils on the glass. The whole family holds their breath when the milk spills or when the eggs break on the floor. Sin has gotten confused with having a runny nose, with not looking ironed, with talking loudly.

This is the kind of hard-edged leadership that ruins lives. You are going somewhere, sure, but it isn't anywhere good. This kind of house grows children who ricochet out of it and swear off eating dinner at the table. Who wants to eat at a table where nothing happens that isn't snarky? Nobody wants to gather around with people who despise you and who see you as a task to be checked off. This is the kind of leadership that does not build culture; it breaks it down. This is the kind of leadership that cripples children. If you are like this, you will find it incredibly easy to have some children that cut with your grain, and one that just always gets on your nerves. When you have blind allegiance to a list, you can come down incredibly harshly and unkindly on a child that just happens to be clumsy, or a little absentminded, or a more tactile learner. This kind of leadership is enormously destructive. It does not matter what is on the table when the people around it aren't at peace. It doesn't matter how clean the house is when bitterness is growing in the hearts of all your children.

So the real goal here should be to illustrate for our children the attributes of both great leadership and faithful following. They should see us setting realistic (but maybe difficult) goals, and working hard toward them. They should see us being visionaries who are anchored firmly in reality. They should see us steadily plodding, faithfully working on things in a realistic way. They should see us laboring hard to make a beautiful life for them while not losing sight of *them* in it.

What I realized was that I needed to make this visionary side of myself a friend of reality. I needed to still want clean bathrooms, but not as much as I wanted peace at home. I needed to want the closets to be organized, but not as much as I wanted my attitude to be organized. I needed to want the table to be beautiful, but not as much as I wanted the people around it to be happy. I needed to set goals that could be attained, I needed to keep an eye on morale, I needed to challenge myself, and I needed to know my frame.

This tension will always exist for us. But, Lord willing, over time, we will learn. We will grow in maturity and faithfulness. We will be able to effectively decide to do something and follow through on it without steamrolling all the people in our path. There is even a chance that sometime in this life I will get that bathroom clean.

CHAPTER FOUR

Panning for Gold

We recently saw a clip of a TV show that was all about men who go panning for gold on the bottom of the Bering Sea. They cut through the ice layer and dive down to the bottom where there is apparently a lot of gold to be found. They use huge vacuum hoses to suck up all the silt and somehow sift it out and separate the gold dust. After quite a lot of this kind of diving and sucking and sifting they melt down all these little bits of gold and come up with something worth a great deal.

What they found and what they ended up with were very different. What they found was a lot of silt with little traces of gold all through it. What they ended up with was a fortune.

My husband brought this up later when we were having a sort of "state of the union" meeting about our kids. He was saying that parenting is like the job of depositing the gold. If our children's lives are the sea floor, we need to leave the gold all over it, everywhere, in little bits.

We can't do it one big nugget. We can't even do it in a bunch of medium chunks. We have to leave gold through their lives in a fine dust that's spread all over everything. At the end of our children's lives, we hope we hope it is worth a fortune. But at any given moment it is the little things that contain the gold.

The gold is quick forgiveness. It is quick repentance. It is cheerful smiles and tender hugs. It is teasing and laughing. It is loving. It is Daddy throwing yet another wrestle party all over the house. It is dinner. Regular. Predictable. It is having physical needs looked after. It is being disciplined. It is being challenged. It is being educated. Being made to do something you didn't want to. It is not being the boss. It is not getting away with lying. It is knowing who to talk to. It is knowing you will feel better when you do. It is security. It is joy. It is every day. It is life. It is knowing your faith, and knowing that it is your parents' too. It is knowing your people and being known by them.

As our children grow, this gold-flecked foundation is being laid. It's happening all the time. It can be very tempting to think that we could just do it once and get it over with for a while. Why must we keep on with this? Wouldn't a big fun vacation once a year be sufficient? Couldn't we just pencil it in? *I'll make up for that harsh remark a little later by letting them have treats. I'll be fun this weekend when I'm not stressed. I'll be better when this weekend is over and we are back to a schedule. I'll be fun over Christmas. I'll be fun when they are older and easier to talk to. I'll be a nice mom when they start being nice kids. I'll think of something really big to make up for this. I'll throw a gold nugget in there sometime, when I have the energy, or the money, or the desire.*

But our opportunities to bless our children are often most present when we least feel like it. This is why we cannot depend on our emotions to dictate our actions. We need to discipline our own emotions to fall in line with obedience. We are to love our children. We are to bring them up in the nurture and admonition of the Lord. That means all the time.

You are busy, trying to accomplish something really important, and children want to help. You are talking on the phone with a friend when a discipline need arises. You could ignore it, or you could get off the phone to lay a little gold. You might be tired when someone wants to tell you a witty story again, just to finesse the delivery. You could sincerely listen and enjoy them, or you could blankly nod.

You are rushing out the door to church, tempted to snap at the whole family for messing up your perfect plan for being ready on time. You could let go of your attitude. You could cheerfully sing with the kids the whole way to church—laying down that little piece of gold that worshipping in fellowship with them matters more to you than showing up on time. That bit of security that you care more what they see in you than what other churchgoers do. Your best opportunities to bestow on your children will almost always be the moments when you least feel like it.

The life of a Christian parent is a life of constant giving, constant depositing, constant building up a bank account of love and security and trust in the lives of your children. The goal is that your persistent investing in them, bestowing on them, and loving them will be so pervasive in their lives that it will simply become a part of their being.

So here is a challenge that truly lives up to that word: When you feel tension mounting—when something is happening that feels extremely wild, when you feel like coming unglued at your children over something that has gone wrong—before you react to them, get a grip on yourself. Look for how you can use this situation to bless them.

Did someone break something that you cared about, that you specifically told them not to touch? How can you bless them in that? Have your children launched a mess that you feel should not have happened? How can you make their lives richer in that? Is everyone desperate to eat dinner and you are still frantically trying to unload the dishwasher so you can start cooking? How can you bestow on them in this—here, now, while you really don't want to? Is someone in your house making a lot of trouble for you? Are they provoking siblings and making conflict? How can you take that situation and nurture them in it?

I know this is hard—believe me. Even writing that paragraph was convicting! I certainly don't mean that when a child is blatantly sinning we should use our highest pitched cutey voice to declare that they are a precious princess while giving them stickers. We are talking about gold here, not glitter.

I mean that we should show them that they are precious by giving them what they need—not what *we* need, or think we need, not what they *deserve*, but what they truly need. We should not be correcting our children in the interest of making our lives easier (although it almost certainly will). Correct them in the interest of making *their* lives richer.

I know that an idea like this will make many parents cringe. *Giving so much to your children isn't healthy! Something about a child-centered home comes to mind.* But giving your own self-control and self-discipline to your children cannot be overdone. Bestowing constant love on a child does not spoil them. It makes them rich.

False love is fool's gold. You can make it look like the real thing. You can hide your selfishness under a pretense of sacrifice. You can discipline in anger. You can demand much of your children, but little of yourself. You can give with lots of strings. You can make your children afraid of your giving while impressing your friends with your selflessness.

But there is something sobering about giving so much. Scripture teaches, "To whom much is given, much is required" (Lk. 12:48). When we give freely to our children, we are constantly raising the bar for them. The more we bestow, the more will be required. Our generosity in this way is not tender sentimentalism.

As we give, we ask God to require. As we bestow, we increase their responsibility. It is not the easy way for us, or for them. When we faithfully strive to enrich the lives of our children in constant, daily sacrifice, we are asking God to ask more and more of them. This is our hope—that our children will be used mightily in the kingdom. This is our hope—that they will in turn give more to their children, that God will require far more of our children and grandchildren than we could ever have given.

CHAPTER FIVE

Discipleship of the Mundane

God likes for His people to be stretched, to be challenged, to be pushed. This is often seen in the fact that we almost never feel like we have things under control. When we finally figure out how to handle one child, we have another. When we think the house is running smoothly, we move. When we feel especially comfortable, we may have to deal with a hard providence. God does not want us to be stagnant, to sit still, to rest on the laurels of success. He has us in training—He is pushing us to grow, to learn, to confess, to rely on Him more, to give more to others, to work harder, to laugh more. This is Christian discipleship.

The hardest part about this is that we have trained ourselves to be people who think in snapshots. We look at a photo of a dreamy home—and extrapolate a whole dreamy life from that one picture. We see calm, clean, simple. We see a life without trouble, without endless piles of shoes by the door. We imagine that everything that happens there is calm, clean, and simple. We want that for ourselves—a life that could be summed up in one little picture of happiness.

The problem with pictures is that they have no direction. They have no goals. There are no obstacles in the life of a photograph. And that is the reason they are so appealing. We look at them and yearn for a life with no growth, a life of arrival. But God did not create us as creatures of arrival. He made us to need to eat all the time. He made us to need to sleep at regular and long intervals. He made us to need to breathe constantly.

You never look at a picture of a beautiful living room and picture yourself in it sleep-deprived with a bad headache and needing to go to the bathroom. You do not envision that Cape Cod getaway as the place the whole family would get the stomach flu.

Oftentimes mothers want this for their real lives. We always want everything to look as if we have arrived, all the time. That is like focusing entirely on the victory moment. Like a football player who never trains, but only practices his touchdown dance. Like a woman who sets beautiful tables for a living, but never feeds anyone. Real life is messy because it is going somewhere. Things constantly need to be done because people are constantly growing. Repetition should not be discouraging to us, it should be challenging.

When we buy into this kind of idealism, we start seeing things as failures that are anything but. Practice drills are not a waste of time. Having another chance to work on things is not a sign of failure. Having room to improve is not something to be sad about, it is something that should encourage and inspire us. God keeps giving me this to do, because this is what He wants me doing. If this is what He wants me doing, then I will do it with my whole being. He gave me the work; I will not back away from it and say it isn't important. I will not sit on the sidelines of this drill and fuss about it.

The funny thing is that we know well that we learn through repetition. We need to practice songs before we can sing them. We need to try something over and over before we have mastered it. We have accepted that part of being human. What we appear not to have accepted is the subject matter. *I don't want to cook for the family again. I don't want to do the laundry again. I don't want to vacuum, to make a birthday cake, to blow a nose, to change a diaper, to pick up toys. I don't want to practice this work that God gave me because, frankly, I'd rather not be good at it.* Because, somewhere in there, we don't like what God has called us to do.

We don't know the value of what we do. We can't always see why God wants us to be doing these things, so we want to negotiate with Him. *Lord, couldn't you think of something better for me to do?* Or worse, rather than complain to God, asking for Him to answer us, we complain to others. We fuss at the children for being what they can't help being. We get dreary to our husbands, explaining yet again how repetitive our lives are. We droop. We make fun of our jobs to ourselves and to others. We belittle our work, we make much of the mindlessness of it, and, not surprisingly, we then lose interest in it.

But imagine we could switch this attitude into a situation where we understand the value of the repetition. Imagine we could see a young girl at a piano, practicing scales with a world-class teacher. Imagine that instead of seeing that she was being taught the fundamentals of something amazing, she was mocking it. Imagine she was complaining and moaning and drooping. Imagine she wouldn't try them. Imagine she was hollering to anyone close enough about how unfulfilling and demeaning this work was, or just sighing to herself continuously. Imagine that she used as her main argument that she was above this kind of fiddly work because she was meant to be a concert pianist.

I would hope that we would all see the foolishness of this kind of attitude. Feeling above it all is simply a way of showing that it is actually above you. We have far more than musical skill to gain by cheerfully practicing the scales that God asks us to. He uses things like this to train us for other things. He wants to see us perfecting the work we are given, cheerfully and willingly practicing when we do not see all the value.

Some women make the opposite error, embracing the calling of motherhood and housekeeping in a mindless way. They act like the scales *are* the concert, like every time their fingers hit the keys, something precious is going on. This isn't exactly the case either. When we honor God in our work, we please Him. We aren't doing this to impress others. We don't need to try. We do not need to justify all the work we are doing to the world, because we are not the teacher. We are the student. We need to trust the teacher, and rest in knowing that our teacher does not make mistakes. He is giving us the perfect things to practice. He is making us into exactly what He wants us to be.

Christian women who seek to honor God as they work through the mundane, repetitive tasks that are given to them will be used for bigger things. We will not be mothers of little children forever. Lord willing, our work will grow with our children. Our challenges will change. Be a faithful student. God is not training you for no reason. Practice. Practice. Practice. But practice with thanksgiving. Practice with joy. Practice with gratitude. Practice with hope.

Our lives do not culminate in a moment. We should not be hoping for one great photo shoot, because that is not what God is doing with us. Our lives are a story—they are interwoven with the next generation in a way that is impossible for us to understand. Getting our sense of achievement and satisfaction out of cheerfully performing the tasks that are asked of us can do nothing but good in our lives. Seeing that God is asking something of you—and delighting in doing it for Him—brings the kind of peace with the mundane that can seem unattainable. You are a Christian. This is Christian discipleship.

Why do you rejoice in making a dinner again? Because God rejoices in your doing it cheerfully, and doing it well. Why can you rejoice in cleaning the bathroom, doing the laundry, running the errands, making the beds? Because God delights in a willing and eager student.

Cheerfully embracing the mundane work in your life, diving into the challenges, working harder than you would think was possible at the little, at the trivial, at the boring—these are all ways to say, "Use me Lord; I am your servant."

CHAPTER SIX

When the Milkshake Runs Low

Have you ever noticed that when there is more than one straw in a milkshake, everyone sucks faster? Everyone knows they are competing, and every sip by someone else means less for you. People start breathing through their noses to minimize lost time.

I have felt for a long time that little children have straws that tap directly into their mom's energy. The milkshake cup is me, and the milkshake is my energy, and every child is armed with a straw. Infants who are either in the womb or nursing have a competitive edge and get to take as much as they want before it even hits the glass.

When the glass is full, things are pretty pleasant. No matter how much milkshake the kids are drinking, there is still some left. It feels pretty good. I am happy to feed them all. But when I'm down to the last inch of milkshake, all the straws start making that horrible noise as they swab around in the bottom of the glass looking for anything they could snag. They all feel the panic of limited supply. They all start getting intense and sucking much, much harder. They are panicked. I am getting panicked. I want everyone to stop so I can have a chance to whip up a new batch. No one stops, because they are trying to get the last of the film off the glass, leaving nothing behind.

The demands for your attention and energy get suddenly loud and obnoxious when you feel like there isn't anything left to give. The truth is, your children aren't demanding anything different than what they were made to need. Usually, when they use this straw, they get fed. Right now, when they use this straw, mom gets snappy.

Of course the ideal would be to never run out of milkshake. To come up with strategies for sensing when it is going to run low. To start noticing what time of day this seems to be happening and taking preventative measures. In a perfect world, we wouldn't even need to think about it because the milkshake would just replenish itself at intervals.

But this is the real world. The real, fallen, messy, difficult world. Every mother deals with having an empty glass and a bunch of straws. Almost every day. And while practice and training and preventative measures might make things flow more smoothly, they won't necessarily make things easier. It is simply going to be hard work.

If you trained as a runner, you would get better and better at running the same race over time. You would speed up. Your form would be better. You would probably enjoy yourself more. But it wouldn't be easy. Professional athletes make what they do look easy. But if they are still pushing themselves, it is still hard.

I think it is common to have this mental ideal of what your days as a mother are supposed to be like. We think that if we were doing motherhood right, then it wouldn't be this hard. Of course there are a lot of ways to improve what we do, to make things easier. But that's like improving a runner's form. You still have to run, and it still won't be easy. You can continue training to the point that you are no longer puking in the bushes and all red in the face by the end of the first block, but you aren't ever going to take the running out of the running.

I was recently talking to my husband about this whole problem of the hard work of motherhood. Why is there almost always a time in the day when I feel like my head may explode, or fall off, or something equally dramatic? He pointed out that the Apostle Paul addressed this very issue when he said, "Therefore, since the race is so easy, and we aren't having any trouble as we try to finish it . . ." It totally cracked me up.

When we are at home with our children, this is the means of our sanctification. This is the testing of our faith. And it is Christ's faithfulness that enables ours. It is our job to cast off sins, to be faithful. It is Christ's job to renew us. We need to be faithful, because He is faithful to us. We can trust Him to fill our milkshakes, because His never runs low.

And just to set the record straight,

> Wherefore seeing we also are compassed about with so great a cloud of witnesses, let us lay aside every weight, and the sin which doth so easily beset us, and let us run with patience the race that is set before us, looking unto Jesus the author and finisher of our faith; who for the joy that was set before him endured the cross, despising the shame, and is set down at the right hand of the throne of God. (Heb. 12:1–2)

CHAPTER SEVEN

The Time Is Now

As our children have gotten older (and as we have gotten more of them), we have become increasingly aware of how short our time is with them. Time is truly flying by. In part, it's because the demands of everyday life are high enough that we are too busy to notice much else. There is always something happening in the next hour, in the next day, in the next few minutes that has our attention. Meals especially seem to roll around the clock at spectacular rates, refusing to be ignored. Some incredibly fast years of my life were made up of the longest days in history.

When I started out on this mothering journey I had a clear vision of what I wanted to be. I could picture the kind of mother that I wanted my kids growing up with. I could picture the kind of home (beautiful, of course), the kind of table (also beautiful, full of wonderful food, and welcoming). I could picture the way I wanted to handle problems with the kids. I would be kind, sincere, loving. I would have lots of time to spend teaching them how to do things like knitting, embroidering, and sewing. We would be hospitable—welcoming people into our beautiful home, because what is another ten guests when you have already made enough pies?

In this future world of mine, I never had to make time for fitness or think about dieting, because magically I never had any baby weight to lose. Because I didn't have any real babies. This future of mine was notable for being entirely free of headaches.

Of course this was easy to plan back when I wasn't actually doing any of it. Setting goals is the easy part. Getting there is what takes some work. Now that I have an intimate knowledge of the work that it would take, should I give them up? Is it time for a little more realism?

I always have a sort of mental list going—things that must be done, things that ought to be done, things that would like to be done, and things that I would like to do. The list jumbles and changes—we squish things in here and there, we make it happen. But one thing that I keep noticing is how little time is actually free. There is no time anymore that is completely vacant. Those embroidery parties with my girls? When? Was I serious? We never finish everything and start looking around for something to do, because something to do is always right in front of us.

This is the thing I've realized lately: If we want to be doing things like this for our kids, we need to be doing them. The time is now. We need to be *now* who we want to be *then*. The future is happening right now. It isn't just bearing down on us faster, it is going past us, too. Some of that future I imagined has already come and gone.

I know that this kind of talk is very depressing for some people. Who you wanted to be and who you are being might be worlds apart. My hope is that instead of this being a sad reminder of what you haven't done, you can use this encouragement to start doing.

As with everything in life, you cannot just *change* it all. God picks us up where we are, not where we should have been. The great blessing of being a Christian is that we have both a reason for the journey that we are on, and a companion for it. We are not alone. We are not striving for acceptance, because we have already been accepted and forgiven.

The point that I am trying to make is that we need to be making the future now, because this is it. You have to have an idea of where you want to be, and then you have to take a step in that direction. Naturally, if you don't know how to cook, you cannot just announce to your family that from this time forth you will make wonderful dinners. You cannot just decide what you want to do, you have to back that decision up with action. Because most things in life aren't really easily come by. It takes work, and discipline too.

I want my girls to be creative and to work with their hands (in addition to having a solid education—just to clarify). I have to teach them, and I have to let do it when it feels less than ideal. I have to be okay with the snippets of yarn and tangled threads that invariably erupt when the girls do. I have to be fine with it happening at funny times and in funny places. If I want these things to be part of our lives, I need to welcome them when they come knocking at awkward moments.

For some mothers this kind of discussion will bring all kinds of things flooding to mind—things that you always wanted to do or be, but somehow forgot about, or gave up on. Some people are naturally eager to do a lot of different things, and may have been storing up an impossible to-do list since early childhood. Others of you might find yourselves wondering why you don't actually have a vision for what you want. You can't think of anything that you really are hoping for in the future. I expect that this is especially common if you come from a broken family, are a first-generation Christian, or never planned on being a mother.

In either case, there are some simple things that you can do to try to get a sense of where you want to be going long term and consequently, what you should be working on now.

For starters, you can ask your husband. You might be surprised at what comes out of that conversation. You might not have known that he would love to have huge Christmas celebrations, and he may never have told you because he didn't want to put that on you, or put the resulting conversation on himself. So if he has ideas, that's a great place to begin.

Another great universal starting point is food. Family cultures vary enormously all over the world, but food is central to all of them. If you don't cook or bake or do anything like that, food is a great place to begin blessing your family. Try to refine a basic recipe that the whole family likes. Perfect your cookies just for them. Work on it. If the first batch of brownies isn't all you imagined them to be, don't throw away the idea. Learn. Grow.

But the most important thing that you can do is start. Once you start, a lot of ideas will become clear to you. I can go for ages without sewing, and then the minute I pull out the machine a thousand ideas come flooding in. When you get your hands into something, your mind often follows with more enthusiasm than you expected.

My husband pointed out recently that fruit is a vehicle for seeds. I love this. It is so true that as we work to bear fruit, we are also bearing the seeds of a lot of future fruit. So, seeking guidance from your husband, or ideas from your children (that should be rich), and blessing from God—dive in.

CHAPTER EIGHT

Home Fires

One of the biggest concerns that many couples have as they head into the years of raising children is that they not lose track of each other. You married this person you fell in love with, and now that a lot of other people have joined you for every moment of every day, it is easy to drift apart. Back in the early days of marriage it was just the two of you. If something was wrong, it was pretty unavoidable. You had to deal with it. But now—now there are a lot of excuses and distractions. Someone else might always need to be talked to first. You can always get absorbed in reading a book to someone, or getting caught up on the laundry. There are a lot of reasons to be tired and just curl up in a ball on your side of the bed and go to sleep fast. And hard.

Does this seem odd? Did God set us up in marriages with the expectation that our initial closeness would lead to us having children, which would drive us apart slowly until they all leave the house and we can't remember ever having been in love with each other? It *should* seem odd, because that is certainly not the plan that God laid out for us. And yet many of us feel like we are on that path and don't know how to get back. We aren't sure what causes this marital distance, or how it could be avoided. In some cases we don't want to avoid it.

The Apostle Paul has some wonderful things to say about marriage and the husband-wife relationship. Ephesians 5:22–24 really spells it out for us:

> Wives, submit to your own husbands, as to the Lord. For the husband is head of the wife, as also Christ is head of the church; and He is the Savior of the body. Therefore, just as the church is subject to Christ, so let the wives be to their own husbands in everything.

A little later, in verse 32, he says, "This is a great mystery; but I speak concerning Christ and the church."

So the husband and wife team is not meant to model a three-legged race, or a relay, or a tandem bicycle. The husband and wife are to model Christ and the church.

When you first get married, chances are good that the wife, all by herself, doesn't exactly look like the church. But given a few years and a few children, that is exactly what she'll look like. Now she is pregnant and has a couple of kids trailing along. Now she is consumed with the business and busyness of others, just like a church. Now her life is full of ministering to others—keeping track of the needy, feeding the hungry, bringing people into fellowship with each other.

But what is the church here on earth *for*? It is here to proclaim the love of God, to bear witness to what He has done for us. Our duty as wives is to help our husbands. Part of that duty is to help our husbands love our children.

Let me hasten to clarify that last little bit. I don't mean that you are to help him love the kids *your* way. I mean that you are to help him convey *his* love to them. When your husband goes off to work, he is loving his family. When he brings home a paycheck, he is loving his family. But if there is no mother taking that paycheck and translating it into hot meals, into clothes for the children, into the comfort of home, then the children may very well not feel that love from their father. It is a mother's job to communicate the love that the father has towards his children. It is our job to translate. When we take the work that our husband does and turn it into fellowship around the table, he is able to enjoy both the fruit of his work and the enjoyment of his love. He provided for us, and we are rejoicing in that.

Nothing about this arrangement would increase the distance between a mother and a father. When you actively seek to carry out the vision that your husband has for your family, you are honoring and respecting him. This is exactly what Scripture tells you to do. You won't be able to do this without his input, and he won't feel afflicted by your questions when they are coming from a framework of respecting him. This is also the kind of conversation that is tremendously healthy in a marriage. What does your husband want to see you working on with the children? Are you asking your husband for decisions about education, about discipline, about the tone of your home? When he gives it, are you arguing? Are you seeking his insight about your mothering? Or do you only ask him in a superficial way that is looking for a compliment? A compliment that had better be gotten or all hell will break loose?

Have you found yourself implementing some big system for cleaning the house or chore charts for the children or anything else that your husband wasn't a fan of? Did you think to yourself that he doesn't know what he is talking about because he isn't here all day and doesn't understand? Did your husband ask you to do something that you simply aren't trying to do? Has he told you that he would love to eat more of something, or less of something, and did you take that request seriously? Has he told you that he hopes to live off of the venison in the freezer when the boys are old enough to go hunting with him? Did you say "Nonsense! We are vegan!" Did he want your children to be vaccinated and you threw down about it? Did he want to give presents at Christmas and you told him that it wasn't godly? That you weren't going to?

These are all ways that you can distance yourself and your home from your husband. But each opportunity like this is not only an opportunity to obey Scripture and your husband, it is an opportunity for the two of you to be growing closer together.

Or, a mother can break fellowship with her husband if he buys the kids donuts (because she recently read something about sugar). The problem here with trying to strong-arm your husband is more than just distancing yourself from his leadership. It is also putting distance between your children and their father. I'm sure that if you found yourself in such a situation as this, you would have your reasons. You would think that it really mattered. That this was super-duper important. But you have lost track of what your goal is. Your goal is to communicate to your children their father's love, not to carry out the regulations laid down by some health blogger. When he does something like this, it should bless you. You should rejoice that your children know their father.

Mothers can get so caught up in the work of providing that they forget whose love they are communicating. They can cut the father out, making him a sort of figurehead with no real influence. We can just run our own show. You can probably easily imagine this happening with a church. A congregation or denomination can get so caught up in the details, in the busyness, that they forget what they are there for. They mention God only in the abstract, and at a distance.

Of course the father can get off course, too—something that Christ simply doesn't do. Since this book is not aimed at fathers, I am not going to try to address the ways that they can sin against their families. But this does not change what Scripture tells us to do as wives (unless there is biblical cause for divorce, in which case you need to be getting counsel from your church elders).

Our first role in the home is as a helpmeet to our husbands. We need his insight, we need his thoughts, we need to be close to him. The absolute best way to maintain your relationship to your husband is to obey Scripture. Honor and respect him within the confines of Scripture. Honor and respect him specifically as you raise your children, because having a right relationship to the father of your children is one of the greatest gifts that you can give your children. If you are doing that, when the children leave your home, you will be closer to your husband than when they came.

CHAPTER NINE

A Table Saved

Food is something that I really enjoy. Not just the eating of it, but the whole story of food. I like to read about, experiment with, and share food. My husband is also a food lover, and so we have always spent fun family time in the kitchen. Of course our children have joined us in this, and we are a whole family of food lovers. I don't say foodies here, because a lot of the time we are not really classy about it.

I mention all this at the outset as a sort of disclaimer that of course this makes the topic of food close to my heart. It is. I love to feed people. And because God has given me this little group of eaters to feed, it is a pretty major part of my life and job description. It is a very simple way for me to dig my hands into blessing my family in a super-tangible way.

But food is more than something that I personally enjoy. It is something that God made important. It is central to our physical lives, and it is central to our spiritual lives.

Food is simply not something that we can opt out of. As mothers, we may have wished we could many times! But preparing and serving food isn't just one of the most repetitive jobs that we have, it is also one of the most powerful.

So much meaning is found around the family table that even the world sees the power of it. There are periodic campaigns to get families to eat together—campaigns based on studies about drug use, depression, obesity, or peer pressure. Families that eat together stay together, as they say.

Who you eat with shapes you on a very basic level. The very act of sitting down and eating together shows a certain level of vulnerability and trust. The word "companion" comes from the Latin *cum* and *panis,* which mean "with bread." In other words, your companions are those with whom you break bread.

But a lot more is happening when a Christian family gathers around a table to break bread together. On a completely physical level, your children are being provided for. They were hungry, here is food. In that extremely simple way it is a means to bless them. The table is often the centerpiece of family time. The evening meal is the one time in the day when everyone sits in one place and does one thing. We fellowship. We see each other. We talk. We laugh. Sometimes we grieve together or celebrate milestones together. The table is a picture of the family.

Even more than that, the table is a picture of our spiritual family. A table is at the center of our worship. Jesus laid a table—a meal of His body and His blood—for us, a very large family, to gather around. This table is a touchstone of our faith. We gather with believers all over the world to partake of this meal. This is a meal that shows us who we are.

Jesus came to this world "eating and drinking" (Mt. 11:19). Far from coming to deliver a series of lectures, Jesus came to feed us, to eat with us, to save us. Jesus came to partake with us. But He didn't come just to partake with us and then leave us as we were. He came to eat with us, to invite us into fellowship with Him, and to transform us through that fellowship.

A wonderful Christian tradition is thanking God before meals. But there is more to saying grace than just a nod to God as the provider of food. We so often rush past things that are familiar to us without thinking of what they mean. If you grew up in a Christian home, chances are good that you pray before a meal out of habit, because it's what you do. But we gather together, every night, even on wild weeknights, for leftovers "in Jesus's name." What does this mean? It means that we are asking Jesus to join us. We are gathered in His name, and we are asking Him to be in our midst. Matthew 18:20 says, "For where two or three gather in my name, there am I with them."

Of course this applies to much more than our dinner tables, but my point is simply that our dinner tables are an important place where this applies. We gather in His name to eat and to fellowship with one another. This makes our table so much more than a place to refuel or chat about the weather. It makes our table a gospel declaration. It makes our table a statement that Jesus came to fellowship with us, and that we are invited to fellowship with Him. This is the good news. Jesus came.

The good news is that Jesus came to fellowship with us as we are. He came for the sick, not the healthy. He came for the snarky moms and the disobedient children. He came to eat with the tax collectors and prostitutes. He did not come to this earth to share an exclusive country club meal with some fancy-pants Pharisees. This is not a reason to panic about the menu plan.

He came to share our box mac and cheese or our beautiful banquet. What is on the table is nowhere near as important as who is around it. We gather to fellowship with each other in the name of our Savior. We are asking Him to be our companion, and a companion of our children. We are asking Him to define who we are. We are seeking His blessing on the little parts of our lives. We ask Him to join us as we small-talk about our days.

Jesus said He came for the sick, not the healthy. But why? To heal them. To fellowship with them, to take their sins, to forgive them, to change them. So when we gather together in His name either at church or in a reflective way around our tables at home, it is not a time to cling to sin. This table is a reminder of that table—of that broken body and spilled blood. This is no place for petty grudges or self-absorption. This is not the time to cold-shoulder the sinners you know the best. This is a time for rejoicing. We are forgiven! We have a Savior!

I can imagine you all wondering what I must be thinking. *Seriously? Have you been to our house at dinner? Everyone is springing out of their chairs and having terrible manners. Sometimes there are still Cheerios from breakfast stuck on the table. The meal amounts to nothing much. Everyone is looking terrible. The one in the high chair is making a spectacular mess. We are a mess. This is not a worship-like celebration. We are not reverent. We are not beautiful.* But you know what you are? You are saved.

CHAPTER TEN

Well Eating

Providing food to people you love is fraught with interesting temptations, many of which we may fall into without even noticing. In this chapter I want to talk about some of these temptations, and a biblical perspective that a mother needs as she negotiates them.

First of all, we must remember that our tables at home are reflective of the table we gather around at worship. As a Christian family, you are fundamentally defined by *that* table, by eating *there*. Now the table that our Lord laid for us with His body and His blood is a table of salvation. It is not a table of guilt. It is not a table of introspection. It is not a table of grievances, of remembering the sins of others towards us. It is a table of forgiveness, of celebration. At a very fundamental level, that table is a table of *gratitude*. We remember the Lord's death until He comes—we remember that we are saved, forgiven, bought, redeemed, and restored into fellowship with God.

Second, there is no other table of salvation. Those who will not come to the table of Jesus Christ can find no peace around a table. This will not keep them from trying to create a table of salvation through their own devising. The Rev. Sylvester Graham made his tasty crackers in an effort to rid us of lust. As though a special cracker could stand in for a savior. The Kellogg brothers were up to some kind of similar righteousness-by-food business. We think this is funny now, in retrospect, because the world has been eating cereal for some time now without any great results, and even graham crackers have failed to solve the problem. But this sort of foolishness did not die with those men, it is as old as mankind, and it is still alive and well. It is sometimes spectacular to see the kind of "righteousness" that can get going in our own times about food.

A few years ago we were stopped at a traffic light near a well-known fried chicken establishment. There were PETA demonstrators outside with a lot of signs denouncing things that have been done to chickens. They were outraged about it, and were asking all of us to use our very basic moral sensibilities and join them in their outrage by abstaining from eating chickens. A very enthusiastic college girl with a big sign was standing right by my window, so I rolled it down and started an awkward conversation:

"Well you had sure better be pro-life! Are you?" She fumbled around a bit and said she was in favor of all life. I rephrased it to clarify that I meant specifically babies in the womb. She got angry, and the guy who was with her laughed at her. The light changed, and off we went.

My point in bringing this up is that, in her world, eating KFC was morally corrupting, but dismembering an infant was simply a choice. You cannot simply take the word of people who are telling you what is good or evil, because, thank God, they are not in charge of that. And when it comes to food, there are a lot of people talking. There are a lot of different billboards on street corners telling us what to do—which ones should we believe? The answer here is *none of them*, because our framework is Christ.

Before the Messiah came, the Jews were bound by the Old Testament holiness code. It provided extensive regulations on food. Food could be unclean for a number of reasons. The wrong kind of animals were unclean. The right kinds of animals, if butchered improperly, were unclean. Unclean people would make food unclean by touching it, and unclean food would make people who partook of it unclean. This was of course the origins of kosher food. In a kosher kitchen, every step of the food preparation must be approved by a rabbi. Many thousands of regulations (which go far beyond the Old Covenant laws) govern the process, and conflict still remains over foods such as gelatin and cheeses. Does this remind you of anything? Have you heard of certain brands being unethical? Have you heard of the origins of food playing a big part in whether or not you should eat it?

When Jesus came, the Jews were anything but comfortable with His treatment of food. Christ was not what they expected, and He did not behave around food as they expected. That's because Jesus turned the laws surrounding food around. He joined tax collectors and prostitutes at a table. In our times, we might think that meant He hung out with the needy people, but in those times what Jesus did was shocking. He did things that would have made any good Jew unclean. He ate with unclean people, and it was highly unlikely that any of the food at Zacchaeus's house was prepared in accordance with Jewish law. But He was not unclean. Instead of the uncleanness being contagious, His cleanness became contagious. Jesus offered salvation to the Gentiles, and it didn't sit well with the Jews. The Jews wanted salvation to be about stuff. About the rules. About the food. About circumcision, about who you were descended from. But Jesus changed all of that. Because of Jesus, no food is unclean. Salvation is found in only one place, and that place is the cross. If Christ has touched us, we are clean. There is no food that can change that.

This is why, at a fundamental level the only way that we can eat well is by being well eaters. And the only way that we can be well eaters is by being made well through the blood of Christ.

Remembering this is so central for our family tables. There is no unclean food; there are only unclean people. Our tables are a place of gratitude. We used to be unclean, and now we are clean. But it is still possible to break fellowship with Christ in how we approach our food and how we behave around our tables. Here are a few ways to do that.

First, we can be fearful. We can spend our time fretting over what we are eating. We can worry that food is one big trap waiting to trick us into cancer, into heart disease, into pasty children with unhealthy guts and developmental problems. This is like the disciples standing on the boat worrying over the waves and the wind. Jesus rebuked them when they finally woke Him up: "O ye of little faith!" *Did you think that this was a problem for Me?* Christian mothers may not be fearful about food, because Jesus is our Savior. He is with us, and He does not want us to fear.

Second, we can be disobedient. We can pursue food interests that our husband does not want us to. We can break fellowship with our husband if he buys our children donuts. We could get so into health food that our husband doesn't feel welcome at his own table. In other words, we could get so consumed with the healthy food that we are no longer healthy people. We could, in pursuit of health, break fellowship with our husbands as well as with Jesus.

Third, we can use food to separate us from others. When we say that we cannot eat with people because of the nature of the food, we are behaving like the Pharisees and not like Jesus. Jesus prioritized table fellowship over food. We relish the "prestige" of being unable to partake in someone else's food. That was not the part played by our Savior, and it was not a part that He admired. You should abhor the thought of using food to identify yourself. What identifies you is the blood of Christ. The Pharisees found themselves abstaining from a table at which Christ was eating, because they were cleaner than that. Make sure that you are not standing with them looking down on the fellowship around anyone's table.

Fourth, we can look to food to save us from the fall. We are all fallen creatures in corruptible bodies. Sin did that, not food. I often hear people bringing up the wholesome past before people used to have illnesses that are common now. The truth is that we all die, and we all die of something. Before pesticides and growth hormones and fertilizers were introduced, people were dying. Perhaps they were dying of wholesomeness, but somehow I doubt that. There is also a lot of consternation about the number of sick people now. Jesus said that He did not come for the healthy but for the sick, and when He came, He did not come with a juice fast. Jesus Christ *was* the solution. And don't try to say that He was talking about just the spiritually sick people. He was known for healing *physical* problems. He came as the Savior of mankind—body and soul. Mankind can not dig out of the consequences of the fall, we can only be carried out. Jesus did that, healthy guts cannot.

I know that I've said a number of things here that might make you bristle. If you are a mother, of course you want to feed your children healthy food. Of course you don't want to sign up for heart attacks and obesity and diabetes. Who would?

Don't read into this that I don't have any problem with any food practices, ever, or that I think childhood obesity is a funny joke. This is not a throw-your-hands-in-the-air-and-don't-care approach. This is a call to care about the right things. I am not saying food doesn't matter. I am saying it matters too much to listen to the wrong people. I am not saying that there shouldn't be change in industries that manufacture foods. I'm sure there should. But it is a change that starts with people being saved. We are like the Jews that wanted Jesus to come in with an army and seize the power from Rome. The Messiah did not save the world like the Jews wanted Him to. He saved it as a *Savior*.

What this means is simple. If we get consumed with the food itself, instead of the Savior who gave it to us, if we think that the fact that we are clean is our own doing, we can change nothing. If we are filled with disgust at the people who are feeding their children white sugar, then we are standing with our own little group of mom-Pharisees looking down on the dirty people.

We cannot change the world if we are not in fellowship with the Savior. And if we are in fellowship with Him—if our lives overflow with gratitude, with joy, with laughter—then there is nothing we can do to keep that from changing the world, because the world will be changed through Him in us.

CHAPTER ELEVEN

Faith Grows

I have the tremendous blessing of being a third-generation believer. My father grew up in a Christian home, both of his parents having been converted before they were married. My mother's parents were converted shortly after she came to Christ in college. But I never knew a time when all of my grandparents were not believers. My grandfather was a pastor, my dad was a pastor, and consequently we grew up playing games like "baptism" in the living room.

Christianity was simply assumed in our house, but it was always alive. It was always being applied to our lives, and not from a distance. There was always the understanding that if the Word of God teaches something, that's what we believe. There was no negotiating with it, ignoring it, or simply choosing to not apply it.

Growing up in this home meant that when we were disciplined, it was about sin. We prayed after being disciplined, seeking forgiveness. We never left the bedroom until everything was right. We grew up with the expectation that we had a personal relationship with Jesus. I was converted at the age of three—hardly a flashy testimony. I was baptized at the age of five. I was saved out of a life of toddler sin, without having had the opportunity to get involved with a gang or anything.

I remember the night that I asked Jesus into my heart as clearly as you can remember anything when you were three. I was in bed, and I didn't like the dark. I started crying about it. My mom came in and said "Rachel, you don't need to cry about it. This house is like a tiny shoebox, and we are all in it. God is everywhere too—even here, so you don't need to be afraid." For the record, the house was almost *exactly* like a tiny shoebox.

I responded "Yes! He is even in my heart." When Mom told me that He wasn't, I was completely horrified! *How had this been overlooked? What needs to be done? Let's take care of this now. Why hadn't they told me earlier?* So I prayed that night, and went to sleep unafraid of the dark. The truth is that I am not really certain that moment was *the* moment. It was when we formalized that I wanted a personal relationship with Jesus, but it wasn't the beginning of my relationship with Jesus.

Years later, when I was maybe in third grade, I had a crisis of faith. I remember being out in the front yard climbing on the tailgate of Dad's yellow truck. I just started to worry about it. *What if I'm not? What if I just think I am going to heaven, but I am not really a Christian?* I remember feeling quite sick about it. I don't know what exactly prompted it, but I was feeling very heavy. After a while of worrying about it, I remember asking Mom, "How do I know I'm a Christian?"

She was working on something else, I think in the kitchen. She just turned and looked at me, smiling, and said, "Rachel! We know you are a Christian! We can see the fruit!"

I don't know if I can communicate to you the level of relief that brought me. *I am not alone in this. They know too. She isn't worried.* After that little crisis, I never wondered again. I never doubted that I was a believer, because I believed.

That one comment from my mom strengthened my faith in a way that she could not have anticipated at that moment. She just encouraged me, but more than that, kept me from a life of doubt.

If she had answered that question really seriously, with concern—if she had said that she did wonder about it since I had lied yesterday, or if she had opened up that door to doubt instead of firmly and cheerfully closing it for me—I know that things would have been different for me. I'm sure that I would have gotten through that, but I probably would have struggled with doubt throughout my life. I would have struggled with doubt because she did. But I didn't because she didn't.

When our children have questions about faith— which they will have—we need to keep this in mind.

There is a way to use your faith to strengthen theirs, and there is a way to use your faith to weaken theirs. Our faith should be a shield to protect our children's faith.

Many parents worry over the spiritual state of their children, thinking that worry and doubt are the only ways to take it seriously. Then the children sin. And instead of disciplining them because it is inconsistent with their salvation, we take it as an opportunity to doubt their salvation. That is a way to attack their faith with our faith (well, actually with our faithlessness).

The faith of your children is like a small tree, and sin can be a windstorm. Faithful parents are friends in the windstorm. They tether off that little tree to their bigger trees. They cannot provide the roots for their child's tree, but they can lend the strength of their own roots.

When you heap doubt and worry of your own onto your child when they are being tested, you are like a person walking past a sapling and giving it a good shake. Just to check if you can pull it out by the roots. Test the strength of that little thing against your own. Point out to it how shallow the roots are. Point out how much deeper your own are.

Because of this strange sort of parental misunderstanding, it is not uncommon to have children professing faith, only to have their parents snort in doubt. It is not uncommon for a child say, "I love Jesus!" and for the parents to respond, "Prove it"—perhaps with more subtle words, but not with more kindness. But when we do this, we are asking their faith to be strong enough to carry the weight of our doubt. We are asking them to be strong enough for the both of us, and that is not feasible for them. Then, as they stumble under the burden of our doubt, we use that as a reason for more. This is not a cycle that builds up the faith of your children. This is a cycle that seems intent on breaking it down.

Of course if your child is manifesting the works of the flesh (Gal. 5:19–21), if they are never in fellowship, if you never see joy, if they are clearly living in the darkness, *then* you need to consider the likelihood that they may not have a relationship with Christ. We don't want to presume that our children are saved just because we are, and they have grown up in our homes and in church. But if you are reading this book, the chances are good that you aren't running the presumptive play. Chances are good that our temptation will be to test the faith of our children instead of building it up.

Once, many years ago, my siblings and I were sitting with a youth group at a camp where my dad was speaking. We didn't know any of these people, and the kids were older than us by a ways. We were sitting in a circle on the floor and the leader asked everyone how old they were when they were saved. As we went around the circle, there were three very sore thumbs. Seventeen. Four. Thirteen and pregnant. Sixteen and a druggie. Three. Fifteen. When the circle was completed the instructor said "I don't think you can become a Christian when you are really little. What do you all think?" And by a show of hands, they agreed that the three of us kids could not have been converted. Fortunate for us that our salvation was not actually something to be voted on! Yet how many parents serve as that group of doubting older children to their own kids?

For many of you, the notion that your children could have faith might be a completely foreign concept. If you are a first-generation believer, it might be hard to see it as a possibility that your little children really do love Jesus: *They are just so naive and don't understand the darkness of sin like I did before I was converted.* Thank God they don't! If you are struggling with doubt, take it to God. Pray over your children and for them. Teach them and nurture them. But lay down the doubt. Cast that on Jesus and not on your children.

CHAPTER TWELVE

Ungraceful Parenting

Many of us come from backgrounds of rigid discipline and high expectations. Others of us may never have experienced house rules, and have no idea how to set them up for our children. It is easy for us to be in one ditch or the other—either all law and no grace, or all "grace" and no law. But the point is really to be somewhere in the middle. How do we do this?

The central thing that we need to see is our own temptations, and to parent in a way that sanctifies us and that fights against those temptations. If you are prone to massive chore charts, laminated couches, and military whistles, maybe your parenting could use a little finger painting and a little laughter. But if you are prone to smile tenderly at a child who is throwing a full-on tantrum, and toss them a cookie, perhaps you should look into disciplining yourself to follow through on something.

Clearly half the battle here is figuring out how you are actually doing now. If your home is a sort of military regime for drones, you could feel like all that ever happens is insurrection and disobedience, because every little step out of the lines you created seems monumental. And you've made so many lines that half the steps your children take are outside them. You might not see yourself as too disciplined, but rather very disordered. When someone suggests that you loosen up, you might think, "What?! We are already going to the bad place in a disobedient hand basket! Loosening up would be the end!" You might think you need to do some serious tightening up, but that will only make things worse.

And if your child is throwing routine tantrums, you might still see yourself as a hard-line parent because sometimes you yell and scream and discipline in anger. But the truth is you are just hard in the wrong way. You need to loosen up in one place, and tighten up a whole lot somewhere else. While other people see you bribing and arguing and threatening and then not following through, you might feel as if you do nothing but discipline. You might think that you follow through because you threaten, or take things away, or generally dislike your children.

Or maybe you think that you are the most generous, kindhearted, and understanding parent around. You think you are ladling on the grace by letting your six-year-old lie down on the floor during church, or your two-year-old "vent his frustrations" and all that by hitting you. You feel like your children will love you because you always give gentle admonitions that are never heard. But anyone else could tell you that your children look unhappy and unloved.

Here is the thing: law and grace are friends. They were always meant to go together. If the law is the skeleton, grace is the flesh. Without the law in there, the grace is just a blob. And without the grace, the law can't move. It can't carry grace anywhere. If there is no law, there is no grace. And without grace, the law is dead. Your parenting needs to represent both the law and the grace to your children.

Think honestly about the law in your family. Do your children obey you? Your first instinct might be to say, "Of course they do!" But think a little deeper than that. When you tell a child to do something, do they do it? Or do they do it after you begin threatening? Do they do it when you start to look serious, or when you stand up? Do they do it after you bribe? Are you bolstering up your commands with dangling carrots or looming paddles? Do you find yourself talking and talking and talking about it? Does it take you twenty minutes to get a child to take a bite? Twenty intense minutes with furrowed eyebrows and raised voices?

What tends to happen with situations like this is that the parents get irritated and end up disciplining. They may still feel like they really enforced the law. But the truth is, they bullied. Instead of simply, cheerfully enforcing a standard, they eventually resorted to force to get their way. That is not the way authority acts. When parents see themselves as an authority, they are enforcing their position, not their personal whims. God wants you to be in authority over your children. He put you there. This is not a position you are striving to get into. You are in it. Act like it.

If you do not have a solid structure of godly authority and law but instead try to just be easy on your kids, the problem you will have is one of boneless grace. You think that you are ladling on the love and acceptance and grace, but you aren't. When God gives us grace, it results in fellowship with Him, forgiveness, and joy.

When we ignore sins our children are caught up in, that is not giving them grace. That has a different name: judgement. Think of Romans 1:24, "Therefore God gave them over to their sins." That was not an example of grace. Sin is like water. Children can drown in even a little bit. Looking away when your kid is stuck in some petty sin is like walking away from a kid who is floundering in really shallow water, and that is not grace. If you love your children, you grab them and haul them out of that danger. You get them all the way out. You don't watch from the house to see if it gets a lot worse. You don't decide that it is their problem, and wish them the best. You don't decide that there will be more time another day to get them out of that water. You don't sit beside the pool and chat to friends or post about it on Facebook. Grace is action.

Grace is not changing your mind about that bite of broccoli because you know you aren't going to win. Grace is not deciding to let a kid stay outside because they stomped at you when you told them to come in. Grace is not deciding that it isn't a big deal that your daughter is yelling at you. Grace is not a coward.

Grace is not a facilitator of sins, it is a solution to them. Good parents have two weapons to help them fight sin on behalf of their children: One is law, and one is grace. The point of both is restoration, forgiveness, and joy. If you don't see those fruits in your home, then you need to reevaluate what you are wielding.

CHAPTER THIRTEEN

Judgey Pants

"Judging" has got to be among the most misused words of our time. Among Christians it is almost certainly in the top five. It is slung around quite fiercely as a magic shield from accountability. It is also often used as an insult: *How dare you judge? Who are you to judge me?* Then there are the people who think they are being wronged by being judged, as though the great burden of our lives is that other people have seen us, and have even formed opinions. *How dare they?*

Of course this kind of consternation applies only to the times when we suspect that other people have formed an unfavorable opinion of us. We don't want them thinking that they have any right to look down on us, or imagining that they could ever do better.

If someone stops by our house coincidentally as we are pulling a pie out of the oven and our children are cheerfully doing chores, and everything that can be seen is beautiful, we welcome the judgment. *Let them look. They will see only the truth.* But if they stop by (as will almost certainly be the case) when the toddler is only wearing snow boots (because she wanted to) and a droopy diaper (because you were going to put her in the shower to get the peanut butter out of her hair before dressing her), and you have not done your hair and makeup . . . You may have an overturned cereal bowl on the floor. The dishes from dinner would be uncharacteristically still in the sink. Any children that are seen would be picking their noses. In *this* kind of instance, we have a lot to say about anyone noticing and learning from any of it. *Do not look at this! It is a lie! I am so much above this it is ridiculous!*

Sometimes we feel guilty for noticing things, as though seeing something in others is a sin. We look away and avert our eyes—not wanting to be thought judgey. We pretend to never notice anything, even if we do. We look away when a friend unkindly corrects a child. We pretend we never heard it—because if we heard it, then they would think we were judging them for it. They might know that we thought that they were wrong. Heaven forbid.

This bizarre level of sensitivity comes from us having a deep fear of negative input. We take the verse "Judge not lest ye be judged" and translate it into "Look not lest ye also be looked at," because we are really invested in having people not look at us (unless, of course, we feel we are looking good). But God does not ever ask us to not look, or to not learn from what we see. In fact, quite the opposite: "Look at the lilies of the field"—what can you learn from them? "Look to the ant"—what can it teach you? "Look at the sluggard"—don't be like that. Avoiding the Proverbs 6 woman is dependent on recognizing the characteristics she has. God wants us to be people who study the things around us and learn from them. It is a way that He uses other people to nourish us. He is constantly putting on little stories around us. We get to see strangers acting out a much more dramatic version of our little sin. If we are paying attention to all the stories that God is telling around us all the time, we will be driven to all kinds of action. You might be embarrassed when your friend is harsh to their child, but were you embarrassed when you did the same thing in the privacy of your own home? See that kind of thing. Apply it to yourself.

Of course part of our unwillingness to read the stories that are all around us is actually an unwillingness to be part of a lesson for others. We don't want anyone to learn something from us that we didn't mean to tell them. This is simply something that shows our pride. We need humility. We need to be willing for other people to learn from us.

And we aren't in charge of the lesson. They might learn what they don't want to do with their children from what we do. They might learn how they don't want to be as parents from us. And that should be fine with us. It might have its embarrassing points, sure. But tough luck! We are all human.

I know that what people see isn't the complete story. I know that some of the times when our parenting is most honoring to God it doesn't look like we are doing very well. It might be one of those church services where our children are all discombobulated and stringy-haired. We might be taking them out every thirty seconds because we are faithfully trying to stay in fellowship with them. It might look to the people behind us like we are having a supremely mess-tastic wreck of a time. But we could go away from there, peaceful in the knowledge that we had honored God. And we could have a service where everyone looked perfect and where we had to repent for being harsh, for whispering threats instead of kindness, all the while intimidating people behind us with our togetherness.

This is the point: we don't know the whole story. We can learn from what we are seeing, and we should, even if the lesson we are learning doesn't represent the whole truth of the situation. This is because we should always know that what we see is incomplete. Many people say that they can't make a judgment because they don't know the whole story. This is such a comic misconception when you really get down into it. *If I knew the whole story, then I could judge.* Oh, really? Could you now? Is that how little you think of yourself? Humility takes the little stories—the little incomplete snippets, and far from judging, learns from them. Pride refuses to see, refuses to acknowledge what God could be teaching us here, because pride wants to be the judge. Humility accepts that what we see is just a tiny bit of the story, a tiny part that we saw for a reason—but that the whole story isn't our business. The whole story is in the hands of the perfect Judge. Pride thinks that if we knew the whole story, then we could be God—as though all that stands between us and perfect holiness is a little information.

Humility sees that what God knows and what we know will never compare, and rejoices in that. But what God shows us in the world and in people around us, He shows to us that we might grow in wisdom. Not so that we might judge, but so that we might discern. That we might grow in grace, grow in repentance, grow in the comfort of our salvation.

We have nothing to fear in the opinion of others if we are right with God. We do not need to run wildly about asking them all to ignore our failings, and pointing at theirs. We are nothing but failings, and neither are they. But if we are right with God—our Judge—we are vindicated. He paid for our sin. We deserved death, and He died in our place.

Jesus is the propitiation of our sins. The Judge saw us as we were, with all of our filth and sin and selfishness, and sent His Son to purchase us. He changed our filth into righteousness, so that we might be justified by His righteousness. He counted His righteousness as ours.

Having been justified through the blood of Christ is our legal standing before God. We are free. But that doesn't mean that we are finished. God wants us to grow. He wants us to learn. He wants us to see, to repent, and to thrive. Part of that is learning from what He is showing us. In the ordinary. In normal life. In the little morality play in front of you at the grocery store. Learning from the things that embarrass you, that make you feel unimpressive. Being willing to be learned from and learning from the people around you.

CHAPTER FOURTEEN

Wound Up

Stress can be a truly difficult problem for anyone. No matter your walk of life, it's a companion. It seems like the whole world is constantly trying to manage, relieve, tame, and organize stress. There are tons and tons of self-help books that offer to show us the magic way to rid ourselves of this problem. Stress might be relatively small in your life, or it might be the one constant, but either way, it is something that most of us would rather be without. It causes headaches, makes it hard to sleep, and adds an element of edginess to almost everything.

I think that one of the world's biggest problems is that sin is fundamentally stressful. There is almost nothing so stressful as the fallout that sin can create. Think of families falling apart—a situation that cannot help but be stressful. Sometimes it isn't anything on a grand scale, it's just the stress of little sin. We pop off at a friend or a neighbor, don't apologize, and then feel afflicted by the tense situation that now surrounds us. Sometimes, to relieve stress, you need to walk right into the storm and get things right.

Of course there are other kinds of stress too—stress that might not be caused by sin, but that tempts us to sin by worrying. You might have a child with an illness, an ailing parent, financial trouble, or difficult people in your family. Sometimes the sin isn't yours, and the fact that you can't confess it for someone else winds you up. Watching other people ruin their lives is certainly stressful. Being a bystander when someone vents their bitterness is stressful. Being the object of envy can be stressful. Being concerned with what other people are thinking about you is stressful. These are the sorts of things that God tells us to cast on Him (1 Pet. 5:7). Do not carry that kind of worry—give it to God. This kind of stress is wonderfully sanctifying when it is dealt with in a way that honors God. Give it to Him. Lift it up to Him. Let Him protect you, provide for you, and give you the grace that you need.

But there is another category of stress that is not connected to your sin, or even to worry. This is the kind of stress that just makes you tired. It can be caused by lots of people pulling on your pant leg, asking for drinks, being anxious about when dinner is coming. It can be compounded by things like a new baby up in the night, a difficult discipline problem, or a lot of mess around the house. It might make you feel emotional, but when you try to sort out what the problem is, you can't pin it down. Nothing is wrong. Oftentimes I will know it's true that nothing's wrong, but I feel so "stressed" because there is so much to do, so much that isn't done.

This kind of stress is simply the ambient noise of faithfulness. This is the kind of stress that you feel right before Thanksgiving dinner. When you could just take a nap instead of slapping together one more pie. But the pie is good. And making it is good. And the fact that your legs ache and your hair is frizzy is just a sign that you have been doing other good things.

What I mean by ambient noise is not just the soothing sound of waves in the background. It is more like you are a basketball player on the free-throw line, and the other team's fans are getting all the noisemakers out. When all that screaming and honking and waving and shouting insults is going on, it doesn't mean that you are doing something wrong. It means that there is a lot of noise in the room hoping you will do something wrong. Some kinds of "stress" are simply what happens when you are being faithful.

This may be taking the athletic imagery too far, but let's do it anyway. What would a coach tell you here? Would they encourage you to really look into the noisemakers? Would they have you listen to noisemakers and practice identifying them? Would they ask you to journal about the noisemakers, asking you to really fantasize about your basketball career without them? Should you be insulted by them? Should you get really into diagnosing triggers and situations during which the noisemakers come out? Should the noise become the only thing that you talk about with others? the only thing that interests you? Should you try to avoid noise altogether and go back to a quiet practice in your driveway? Of course not.

Every good coach would want his players to be strong in the fundamentals. Don't come to a standstill and hold your ears at the first honk of a random kazoo. Don't freeze up on the free-throw line. Remember the basics. Look at what is happening right here, right in front of you. Do what you know how to do here. Now.

Part of the point of practicing free throws in exactly the same way every time is that you are building muscle memory. Habits. You have a system, a rhythm. You do it the same way every time so that when the stakes are high and the pressure is on, and the people are all waving the big long balloons, you don't even have to think about what you are going to do. This is because the ambient noise doesn't matter—the background whistles aren't your job. Your job is right here, and you know how to do it. All the noise isn't a reason to stop doing what you are supposed to be doing.

Someone once said, very wisely, that we need to imitate the psalmist: We need to spend less time listening to ourselves, and more time talking to ourselves. Like the psalmist saying, "Oh my soul why are you grieving? Why disquieted in me? Hope in God, your faith retrieving, He will still your refuge be" (Ps. 42). He is giving himself a pep talk. He is counseling himself with what he knows to be true in a time that doesn't feel smooth.

For many of us the stress in our regular lives is actually quite manageable, if we concentrate on the fundamentals. Stress confuses. Sometimes the very fact that something feels stressful makes us assume something is wrong with it, or with us. Sometimes when stress hits, you feel like you can't see straight, or think your way out of a paper bag. Sometimes we get so muddled that we aren't sure what we were doing on the court in the first place.

The way out of this kind of stress is not a way to keep stress from ever being in your life. The goal (in spite of what the world thinks) is not to arrive a perfectly stressless place. The point is to be the kind of faithful that works through stress in a way that honors God. The way to deal with this kind of stress is to see through it. To focus your mind on the task in front of you. Because even if you are unable to formulate a clear bullet list, you can figure out the biggest priority. No matter what the situation is, there is one perfect answer every time. Obey.

Make obedience your fundamental. If you prioritize obedience, everything else will fall into place. Prioritizing obedience in the face of stress is a wonderful way that to disarm it. Often times we might think that it is too hard to tell what obedience would be in some particular complicated situation, because it is so tangled. When you feel hopelessly wound up and stressful, go back to your fundamentals. Obedience starts with what is right in front of us. Pick up any little sins you see lying around. Have you been complaining? Have you been ungrateful? Have you been unkind to your children, or fussy to your husband? Have you wanted other people to think of you, but been unwilling to think of others? Have you indulged yourself by wallowing in the stress and enjoying the drama, but forgetting the task?

We can always obey, and God always provides the grace. The fundamentals are always right in front of us, and they are always the same. Love God, hate sin.

CHAPTER FIFTEEN

A Little Morning Rugby

Some of our children are now in the age range where we can say things like, "Go put on your pajamas" with the reasonable expectation that it will happen. This was not always the case, and it wasn't without a lot of sweaty eyeballs that we got here. We put in the years of stuffing people into their footie pajamas and buckling every car seat buckle by the sweat of our brows.

As our children have gained a level of capability, they have also gained a certain kind of power over how the morning goes. What used to be a parent-only performance has now expanded to include several others. What I mean is that once a child is capable of putting on their own pants, they can now neglect to do it. Or they can do it so slowly that they might as well have not done it. There are all kinds of opportunities for our children to throw off the morning plan simply by being slow, not listening, getting droopy, or failing to do the simple tasks you gave them.

If you have ever been in this position as a parent, I think you know what happens next. The whole morning takes on an aura of conflict. Usually you are in a hurry, and usually the kid involved does not feel the pressure of it like you do. Usually something that was very inconsequential kicked it all off, like a kid who is supposed to be brushing their teeth wandering in to tell you about something they dreamed about. You probably cut them off, sent them away with a stern admonition to *do what I told you right now turn around go back stop it and pay attention.* They probably wander back to brush their teeth, but this time feeling picked on. Feeling like no one cares or wants to talk to them. They start having a hard time with everything. They can't find their shoes even though their shoes are where they always are. They get another stern "use your eyeballs" kind of remark. Because they are in the frame of mind to feel picked on, this hurts too. Then you find them lying on the living room floor. Their defense is that they were just putting on their socks. You are probably not thrilled with their system, and tell them as much in passing—*sit up right now put your socks on get your shoes on already act your age come on!*

When this happens at our house, it is normal for nothing to have gotten truly horrendous, but for everything to have gotten just a bit bad. This is the kind of situation where I could almost bet that someone will get their finger shut in the car door. It is just the way these things go. It also doesn't happen all the time, and so when it pops up I am often not prepared for it.

But during the whole stretch of a morning like this, chances are good that everyone is playing the part of the victim. When you are the mother who washed all the clothes, got everyone bathed, has the clothes laid out for them, and you simply want them to connect the dots—dots they are more than capable of connecting—it is easy to feel as if the children's sudden phantom troubles with various things are motivated by deliberate malice toward you. You get defensive. *This is not my responsibility! I did my part!* They are the ones who get the blame. But usually, placing blame does not result in discipline, because you are in a big hurry and not taking the time to actually deal with the problem. Also, you usually know that discipline would be out of line, because at some level you recognize that you are being harsh, unkind, and demeaning. So the issue doesn't get resolved, you just all manage to get in the car one way or another and go peeling off to church or school.

We have been working through this at our house—looking for some simple solutions that will help us all keep in order and in fellowship as we are trying to get our many people together and out the door. This kind of thing doesn't happen without teamwork. We are asking our kids to be part of the team. *It is time for you to do your part and help us get out the door on time.*

Titus, at the age of four, recently got his first introduction to team sports at a rugby clinic. At one point his coach started some kind of a drill and threw the ball to Titus. He was not expecting the throw, and the ball hit him in the face. He was quite brave about it, and it was not a big deal, but it reminded me of what happens sometimes in the mornings.

We want it to be flawless teamwork. We want to just chuck the rugby ball at one of our kids and have them be ready to catch it and run. We are expecting their hands to be up, to be engaged in the drill. But, since they aren't, it beans them in the nose. Then, as their eyes are still watering and their whole face is stinging, we start throwing more. *Try again! What is your problem? Try again! You still aren't catching it? What is wrong with you? You are big enough to catch!*

The trouble is that no matter how easy that first toss was, if it hit someone in the face, you can't ignore it. At this point, effective coaching, coaching that is actually interested in people learning, will stop to make sure that everyone knows what is going on and is ready for the next ball. This might mean that you have to stop and discipline for something little, perhaps for not having had those hands up and ready in the first place. But no matter what, you need to get it all the way right and stop the nose from stinging before another ball is thrown.

This is just another example of a parent's need to be a good leader. You need to make sure that all of your children know what you expect. You should not have silent expectations with consequences of resentment from Mom. Lay your expectations out clearly, and enforce them clearly and cheerfully.

The truth is that if your kids are old enough to be doing jobs by themselves, they get satisfaction out of that ability. They want to feel effective and capable. When we belittle them with comments like, "Can't you even figure out how to get your coat on without me?" we aren't helping. This is not motivational. This is not leading effectively. Dragging everyone somewhere is not leadership, it is bullying.

Expect a lot of your children, but never more than you expect of yourself. If the first thing that doesn't go smoothly sets you off in a chain of fussing and demanding, blaming everyone but yourself, you need to recognize how your children are simply following you. They are imitating your problem-solving skills. They will in all likelihood start blaming, demanding, and fussing. *She is in my way. I can't get in because my leg itches. But no one said when they handed me this belt that I was supposed to put it on!*

They can't find their coat, because you can't find your patience. They aren't motivated to obey you cheerfully because you aren't motivated to cheerfully obey God. You are indulging yourself, and so are they.

But if you take responsibility for all the aspects of the situation, you will find that you have far more responsible help. If you are clear and calm, your children will be clear and calm when someone is sitting on their socks.

If you are able to prioritize fellowship and obedience, they will too. There will not be a frantic blame-festival in your home.

Good leadership is engaged and involved the whole time. It is clear about expectations and consistent about consequences. But good leadership always starts with the leader. It always starts with what you expect of yourself. If you are engaged in disciplining yourself, your children will know. They will mimic that. They will want to follow.

CHAPTER SIXTEEN

Popping the Weasel

I truly believe that one of the greatest skills a mother can have is a sense of humor. Laughter does all manner of things on a physical level, making you feel better by releasing endorphins and also by reducing the levels of stress hormones.

But laughter is more than that. Proverbs 17:22 says, "Laughter does good like a medicine, but a broken spirit drieth the bones."

Laughter heals. A broken spirit makes things worse. There are a lot of times in the life of a mother when these could easily be your two choices—laugh or break. Let your spirit lift you up through laughter, or let it dry you out through taking itself seriously.

You know the day that you wash all of the bedding, even the comforters? Probably causing a traffic jam of other loads that needed to go through? You know what will happen, right? Almost guaranteed puke in the night, or at least an accident, possibly a bloody nose. If you wash it, it will be the victim of some kind of catastrophe. What is this kind of thing other than funny? It is slapstick-level comedy, with the clean sheets playing the role of the pane of glass. Can you laugh? Or do you let it dry you out just a little bit more?

Although our lives abound with physical comedy when we have children, they also abound with a sort of spiritual comedy. With little children, when sin has not had a chance to grow up big, it is often funny: petty squabbles, hilarious accusations, outrageous justifications for selfishness, and so on. Recently our two-year-old started making a pig noise that was so powerful that it surprised her. She turned it into a dragon noise, to be used while chasing the older kids around as "dragon-girl." Now dragon-girl was a perfectly happy and sweet little thing who liked to play, run fast, and laugh. But a few days after the release of happy dragon-girl, selfish dragon-girl came out. This was the spontaneous result of a moment of fury: "Gimme that! Gimme that! It's *mine!* Snooooooort!" It was so pricelessly funny. What is selfishness other than a pig and dragon mix anyway?

This was sin. It was ugly selfishness. And it was also hilarious. So what is a parent to do? Is laughing wrong? Of course not. But it would be if the laughing took the place of the dealing with it. That kind of sin, no matter how funny, is a real threat to your child. So take it seriously enough to not let it go, but lightly enough to find it funny.

In our house, we make a point to discipline only when we have a biblical name for the offense, because we want our children to know that what we are doing is enforcing God's law. So they would know they are being disciplined for disobeying their parents, not splashing in the sink. But this does not keep us from having a number of nicknames for sins, treating them like the old friends and casual acquaintances they are. There is the *boss and block*, a play that is traditionally run when you are feeling unkind towards a sibling but can't risk engaging them face-to-face lest you be caught. Oftentimes it is used in doorways—hands on the frame, blocking the entry of the sibling, using your buns to prevent them from coming through. This one is used under the pretense of "I didn't know she was there, so how could I have known that I was in the way?" It is often used to great effect in getting in the car so as to make the most difficult possible entry for others.

Freelancing is another well-known behavior in our house that usually involves unauthorized rummaging the fridge, maybe the sink, and possibly the craft supplies. There is *losing the bubble*—an ancient system for getting emotional when something goes wrong for you. Then there is *throwing the bubble*—which is what you do when you are trying to dramatize what someone else did to you or the situation that afflicts you.

There are *grabby-pantsing* and *fussy-bussing*. There is *'tude doggin' it*. There is *fat-facing*—showing no emotion at all while pulling your face back in retreat.

Make a double chin and dead eyes. Now you've got it. One of my personal favorites was when I overheard Daddy counseling someone about the *drama mayonnaise* on their *fussy sandwich*. And there is the *freeze up*, also called the *stick in the mud*, whose popularity depends on personality type.

The fact that we joke about these things—with the offenders, expecting them to laugh about it too—does not mean that we aren't taking the offenses seriously. We are taking them seriously, as witnessed by the fact that we are talking about them. Sometimes the laughing about it doesn't happen until after you have retrieved the child from the grip of the sin.

The way I think of it is like a garden. The sin in our lives is like weeds coming up. When you see them, you pull them up. Our children are with us, learning how to tend their gardens. There is nothing wrong with having a casual relationship to the tiny weeds you are pulling out. If they just came up, they can be joked about as you pull them up. It is okay, so long as you are pulling them up.

Parents often feel so foolish trying to take a little sin seriously and trying to get their children to take it seriously, that they give up. They are trying to persuade their kids that this little tiny baby weed is a *really* big deal and we have to pull it up! But when their child doesn't see it, they lose the vision themselves, and just let it go. Sometimes they discourage their children by constantly freaking out about the tiny weeds until their children just glaze over and space off. They figure that when it is much taller they will deal with it. But this is not good gardening (or good parenting). Putting it off will not just make it easier to identify the weeds, it will make it harder to identify the plants.

A little humor goes a long way toward lightening the mood as you and your children spend the days in the sun pulling weeds. When you find a little weed, and you are on your knees with your gardening gloves on, this is not a time for weeping. This is a time for action. *Got it!*

Make sure that your children understand this. Cheerful work on the little weeds is basic Christian living. Getting out there every day to see what is coming up and deal with it is faithfulness. The fact that the weeds are coming should not surprise us. Humor in this kind of setting is simply a "whistle while you work" mentality.

Certainly, if you have an eighteen-year-old who is now completely overshadowed by the weeds, there is nothing funny about it. I am not recommending teenage pregnancy or meth use as a great joke for a little family slapstick. But if your children are little, chances are the sin they struggle with is still mostly little. This is not a reason not to worry about it, but a reason to work on it persistently and deliberately. But the work is the kind of work that is at its most effective when the morale is high, and one great way to keep the morale high is to keep your sense of humor. Laugh often. Work joyfully.

If you tend to be a serious person, this may strike you very wrong. *She is talking about sin in a lighthearted fashion. But it is sin! Sin is why Jesus had to die on the cross! This is no laughing matter.* This is all very true, if Jesus were still on the cross. But He isn't. He was victorious! He redeemed us from all of that. To be very serious about sin is a way of being reverent toward it. But being reverent toward sin is actually being irreverent about forgiveness. Being serious about *dealing* with sin is honoring to God, because it is being serious about forgiveness.

So yes, I am "lighthearted" about sin—because what else, in a very literal sense, is a Christian to be? Our hearts are made light by the one who died with our sin and overcame death. But just like Christian in *The Pilgrim's Progress,* our hearts are not light until we lay down our burden at the cross. Put it down. Faithfully drop it. Do not carry your sin about with you, and do not carry your children's sin about with you. Do not spend all your time rummaging around in your sin-bundle that is already at the foot of the cross. Do not teach your kids to do that either. If you laid it there, you are lighthearted. If you cannot feel lighthearted, you need to lay down your burden.

CHAPTER SEVENTEEN

The Long-Term View

Whenever you take on any kind of project, you will run into obstacles. This is especially true of things that will, by necessity, take a long time. Think of losing weight and getting fit. Think of getting organized, redecorating, or teaching yourself some new skill. When facing a long-term project, it is easy to get distracted, it is easy to lose your motivation, and it is easy to change your mind. Maybe you lose three pounds and feel better so you start eating cookies again. Maybe you decide the new skill doesn't really suit you, or it makes a mess, or it is frustrating, so you give up.

But what if this long-term project is other people? What if you started out all motivated about having children, but now you are tired, frustrated, and feeling lost? In healthy Christian communities there will be young people growing up with an admiration for the work of raising children. It is easy to stand on a hill looking out over all the landscape and see the destination far away in all its beauty. It is easy to see why this is a glorious calling. It is easy, because the view is clear. Many young couples start out their parenting journey with a clear, happy, optimistic perspective. They see, off in the distance, the heavenly city. They cheerfully say, "Yes! Give us some children to take there!" Even the shadowy parts look pretty from the top of a hill. *They just add shading! What a beautiful, textured view on the way to this heavenly city!* They can hardly wait to get started.

One of the inevitable troubles parents will face on this long term journey is discouragement. Once you set out on the actual work of walking through the countryside to get there, it isn't always scenic. Sometimes those things that seemed inconsequential from afar turn out to be rather huge obstacles when you get close up. Sometimes you get down in a valley and you can't see your destination anymore, because hilltop views are not what hiking is made of. Sometimes you just flat out don't want to walk up that hill. Sometimes you realize that you were crazy-naive about this trek when you set out, that you didn't prepare adequately, that you aren't enjoying yourself, and maybe even that you aren't a very good traveler. That is what discouragement feels like. It feels like you haven't caught a glimpse of your destination in a long time. It feels like maybe you didn't want to go anyway, or maybe you aren't skilled enough to get there.

I think we all know what it feels like when nothing seems to be working well. Suddenly all the kids are going through a fussy stretch at once. Maybe they have started back-talking more or bickering with each other. In a mother's life, new sin sprees from the kids can seem like someone flipping over spiritual rocks. *Let's see what Mom has under this frustration rock! We haven't tried this one before! Let's see what bounty of centipedes she keeps under here! Maybe we can rustle something out that will startle her as much as it does us!* And thus you can find that one of the biggest sources of discouragement in your mothering life is yourself. Maybe you never pictured yourself as someone who would get seriously selfish about sleep. Maybe you always thought you would do lots of crafts with the kids when you had them, but now your blood pressure rises at the sight of a glue stick, not to mention scissors. I don't think I need to go into too much detail on what this feels like, because I imagine we all know too well. Some of you may feel like this is your only mode of mothering. Like you never do get a glimpse of where you are going unless it is the view down into yet another valley.

But low points and discouragement are actually a perfectly normal part of the job. We are human. This is hard. You can't head out on a long journey over rugged countryside and expect the whole thing to be something like a fevered dream from the creators of My Little Ponies. The thing that distinguishes unbelief from belief is how we deal with discouragement and fatigue. We are

Christians. God has provided for this. Faithfulness does not pitch camp in the valley. It does not decide to settle down in the swamp because the hill is steep. Faithfulness obeys. It presses on. It trusts. It remembers.

One of the most beautiful things is how obedience and encouragement go hand in hand. Obey, and God will strengthen your steps. Act in faith, and He will reveal the path. When you look to God for direction, He always provides. We have a compass. We know the way. Sometimes, the way seems like an impossible scrabble on hands and knees, but that is not the same thing as being lost.

Practically speaking, when you have a posse of little kiddos on your hands, there will be times when you don't know what to do. There will be times when the little problems mount up into something a lot more intimidating. Faithfulness takes a step. And then another. Faithfulness recognizes that this is a tricky part, and begins moving to get through it. We have had times with our children where the feeling of need is overwhelming. But when we ask God for direction on each of the little things, not only is direction provided, but progress is made. Sometimes, you need to ask God to show you each little foothold. That is not a sign that you are failing. It is not a sign that you will never find your way out. It is a sign that you are still on the journey, still obeying, and that you know who to ask for help.

When discouragement comes on a mother, the temptation is to vent. To change the subject. To do anything but take a step. We might want to sit down and brainstorm about the itinerary for next week. We might want to tell ourselves that no one else is making progress, either. We develop bad attitudes about the people who appear not only to know the way, but have gone so far as to pack snacks and raincoats. But none of those things is obedience. Obedience is bigger than discouragement, and the two can not live side by side. When you need encouragement, obey. When you are tired, walk. When you feel lost, remember. The more you discipline yourself to overcome discouragement with obedience, the less discouragement there will be to overcome.

CHAPTER EIGHTEEN

It Ever Shall Be

One of the most common struggles that women seem to have with their job as mothers is the constant temptation to be discontented. There is always going to be something wrong. Maybe the house is too small or the kids are too rowdy. Maybe you are tired of cooking or annoyed with the laundry. Maybe your children are being disobedient or they seem fussy all the time. Maybe you feel unappreciated and spend time thinking about how others should be treating you. These are all ways of saying *this job is too hard for me, and I am not satisfied in it.*

Strangely, we have also bought into the lie that our job is not valuable or challenging. We are very conflicted in our complaining. The job is both too hard and also too easy. What an odd way to go about saying that it is just perfect for us. We are like Goldilocks tasting the porridge, only instead of settling on one that is just right, we are calling it both too hot and too cold. At the same time. Then we sit down with it, but spend all our time looking to our left and to our right, at this one's serving or that one's bowl. *Something anywhere but what I've got and where I am would be good. I am so unfulfilled because I am so needed here. I am so tired because this work is not worth my time.*

The feminist agenda was spectacularly effective in persuading women everywhere that this job—this staying at home and caring for children—is the work of unambitious and boring women. And strangest of all, many women who willingly choose to do the job have believed the bad press. *Yep, yep. Job for losers. That's what I do.*

Discontent will never change the world. If you want your work to have a lasting impact on the world, define yourself with gratitude. Be thankful over the laundry. Be thankful when you find yourself nursing a baby in a carload of hungry children. Be full of gratitude, not only for the cute photo opportunities that will come your way as a mother, but over the accidents and snotty noses and dirty floors. Give thanks for the sticky juice rings on the counter. Give thanks for the milk spill, for the stomach virus, for the pants that are too tight after that last baby.

I don't know if you have ever tried singing a hymn or a psalm when you are feeling grumpy, but if not, you should. If you haven't (and if you aren't currently grumpy so you can't try right now), you will have to take my word for it that it is transforming. You can either sing the hymn or have the attitude, but there is not space for the two things at once.

Gratitude is like that. It transforms. It is such a force that it cannot coexist with selfishness, with discouragement, with discontent. When you are thankful for what God gave you to do, you are fit to do it. When you are thankful for the things that are right in front of you, getting in your way and messing up your hair, you are at peace with God's will for your life. And of course when you are at peace with God and with His will for your life, you are equipped to do great things.

Gratitude doesn't transform just our moods. In a very real way, gratitude is a force of change in the world. When you thank God for the filthy laundry that is in front of you, you are not motivated to walk away. Getting your attitude straight equips you to deal with things in an effective way. Being thankful for the problem is often the first step of the solution.

Our gratitude for our problems does not just enable us to troubleshoot more effectively, or get through the day with fewer emotional headaches, although it does do those things. Gratitude enables us to do our daily work as unto the Lord. It makes the little things that we do every day an offering to God. When we do the dishes, when we correct the children, when we mop the floors, when we sort out the clothes and clean out the basement. When we do all these little things full of gratitude, we are making a difference in the kingdom of God.

In our church, at the conclusion of each worship service, we sing the "Gloria Patri" with our hands raised. We lift our hands in a gesture of lifting our worship up to God, but also a gesture of lifting the work of our hands up to Him. Asking Him to use the things that we do in the course of the week for the kingdom. We lift up the hands that have been in the sink with the dishes, hands that have been fixing hair and buttoning pants, hands that have been wiping off the table and driving to school, hands that have been changing diapers and tickling tummies, hands that have been busy holding other hands.

These hands, this work, Lord, take them. And when I look down our row at church, I see that God has multiplied the work of our hands. All these little hands raised to Him. Offering up their coloring and schoolwork. Offering up their staying in bed at nap time. Offering up their laughter, their joy, and their lives. And I know, beyond a shadow of a doubt, that there is nothing better or more powerful that I could be doing with my hands.

Glory be to the Father,
and to the Son, and to the Holy Ghost.
As it was in the beginning, is now and ever shall be,
world without end, amen.